100

Hadiths for Kids Ages 7-9

(From the Book of Al-Bukhari)

Eman Publishing
P.O. Box 404
FISHERS, IN 46038
USA

www.emanpublishing.com

Order Online: www.SuperChargeHomeSchooling.com

ISBN 13: 978-1-935948-20-9

LCCN: 2011942391

EMAN
publishing

Cover Design by SuperCharge HomeSchooling

Printed in the United States of America

100

Hadiths for Kids Ages 7-9

(From the Book of Al-Bukhari)

Dedication

*'(Our Lord! Accept this from us. You are
the All-Hearing, the All-Knowing).'*

(The Qur'aan: Chapter 2, Verse 127)

Hadiths from the Book of Belief:

1.   Narrated by Ibn 'Umar (radi Allahu anhu): The Prophet (Salallahu alayhi was salam) said,

"Islaam is based on (the following) five (principles):
   1. To testify that none has the right to be worshiped but Allaah and Muhammad is the Prophet of Allaah.
   2. To offer the (compulsory congregational) prayers dutifully and perfectly.
   3. To pay Zakat (i.e., obligatory charity).
   4. To perform Hajj (i.e., pilgrimage to Makkah).
   5. To observe fast during the month of Ramadhaan."

2.   Narrated by Abu Hurayrah (radi Allahu anhu): The Prophet (Salallahu alayhi was salam) said,

"Faith (Belief) consists of more than sixty branches (i.e., parts); and *haya* (This term "*haya*" covers a large number of concepts which are to be taken together; amongst them are self-respect, modesty, bashfulness, and scruple, etc.) is a part of faith."

3.   Narrated by 'Abdullaah bin 'Amr (radi Allahu anhu): The Prophet (Salallahu alayhi was salam) said,

"A Muslim is one who avoids harming Muslims with his tongue and hands. And a *Muhaajir* (emigrant) is the one who gives up (abandons) all what Allaah has forbidden."

4.   Narrated by Abu Musa (radi Allahu anhu): Some people asked the Prophet (Salallahu alayhi was salam),

"Whose Islaam is the best? (i.e., who is a very good Muslim)?"
He replied, "One who avoids harming the Muslims with his tongue and hands."

5.   Narrated by 'Abdullaah bin 'Amr (radi Allahu anhu): A man asked the Prophet (Salallahu alayhi was salam),

"What sort of deeds or (what qualities of) Islaam are good?"
The Prophet (Salallahu alayhi was salam) replied, "To feed (the poor) and greet those whom you know and those whom you do not know.

6. Narrated by Anas (radi Allahu anhu): The Prophet (Salallahu alayhi was salam) said,

"None of you will have faith till he wishes for his (Muslim) brother what he likes for himself."

7. Narrated by Abu Hurayrah (radi Allahu anhu): The Prophet (Salallahu alayhi was salam) said,

"By Him in Whose Hands my life is, none of you will have faith till he loves me more than his father and his children."

8. Narrated by Anas (radi Allahu anhu): The Prophet (Salallahu alayhi was salam) said,

"None of you will have faith till he loves me more than his father, his children and all mankind."

9. Narrated by Jarir bin Abdullaah (radi Allahu anhu):

"I gave the pledge of allegiance to the Prophet (Salallahu alayhi was salam) for the following:
1. Offer prayers perfectly
2. Pay the Zakat (obligatory charity)
3. And be sincere and true to every Muslim.

10. Narrated by Anas (radi Allahu anhu): The Prophet (Salallahu alayhi was salam) said,

"Whoever possesses the following three qualities will have the sweetness (delight) of faith:
1. The one for whom Allaah and His Prophet become dearer than anything else.
2. The one who loves a person and he loves him only for Allaah's Sake.
3. The one who hates to revert to atheism (disbelief) as he hates to be thrown into the fire."

11. Narrated by Anas (radi Allahu anhu): The Prophet (Salallahu alayhi was salam) said,

"Love for the Ansaar is a sign of faith and hatred for the Ansaar is a sign of hypocrisy."

12. Narrated by 'Umar bin Al-Khattab(radi Allahu anhu): I heard the Prophet (Salallahu alayhi was salam) saying,

"The reward of deeds depends upon the intentions and every person will get the reward according to what he has intended. So whoever emigrated for worldly benefits or for a woman to marry, his emigration was for what he emigrated for."

13.   Narrated by Abu Hurayrah (radi Allahu anhu): The Prophet (Salallahu alayhi was salam) said,

"The signs of a hypocrite are three:
1. Whenever he speaks, he tells a lie.
2. Whenever he promises, he always breaks it (his promise).
3. If you trust him, he proves to be dishonest. (If you keep something as a trust with him, he will not return it.)"

14.   Narrated by Abu Hurayrah (radi Allahu anhu): The Prophet (Salallahu alayhi was salam) said,

"Whoever establishes the prayers on the night of Qadr out of sincere faith and hoping to attain Allaah's rewards (not to show off) then all his past sins will be forgiven."

15.   Narrated by Abu Hurayrah (radi Allahu anhu): The Prophet (Salallahu alayhi was salam) said,

"Whoever observes fasts during the month of Ramadhaan out of sincere faith, and hoping to attain Allaah's rewards will have all his past sins forgiven."

16. Narrated by Abu Hurayrah (radi Allahu anhu): The Prophet (Salallahu alayhi was salam) said,

"If any one of you improves (follows strictly) his Islaamic religion then his good deeds will be rewarded ten times to seven hundred times for each good deed and a bad deed will be recorded as it is."

17. Narrated by Abu Mas'ood (radi Allahu anhu): The Prophet (Salallahu alayhi was salam) said,

"If a man spends on his family (with the intention of having a reward from Allaah) sincerely for Allaah's Sake then it is a (kind of) alms-giving and reward for him."

18. Narrated by Sa'd bin Abi Waqqas (radi Allahu anhu): The Prophet (Salallahu alayhi was salam) said,

"You will be rewarded for whatever you spend for Allaah's Sake, even if it were a morsel which you put in your wife's mouth."

Hadiths from the Book of Knowledge:

19. Narrated by 'Abdullaah bin 'Amr (radi Allahu anhu):

'Once the Prophet (Salallahu alayhi was salam) remained behind us in a journey. He joined us while we were performing ablution for the prayer which was over-due. We were just passing wet hands over our feet (and not washing them properly) so the Prophet addressed us in a loud voice and said twice or thrice: "Save your heels from the fire."'

20. Narrated by Ibn 'Umar (radi Allahu anhu): The Prophet (Salallahu alayhi was salam) said,

"Amongst the trees, there is a tree; the leaves of which do not fall, and it is like a Muslim. Tell me the name of that tree."
Everybody started thinking about the trees of the desert areas; and I thought of the date-palm tree but felt shy to answer. The others then asked, "What is that tree, O Allaah's Apostle?" He replied, "It is the date-palm tree."

21. Narrated by Ibn Mas'ood (radi
Allahu anhu):

The Prophet (Salallahu alayhi was salam) used
to take care of us in preaching by selecting a
suitable time, so that we might not get bored.
(He abstained from pestering us with sermons
and knowledge all the time).

22. Narrated by Anas bin Malik (radi
Allahu anhu): The Prophet (Salallahu
alayhi was salam) said,

"Facilitate things for people (concerning
religious matters), and do not make it hard for
them and give them good tidings and do not
make them run away (from Islaam)."

23. Narrated by Ibn 'Abbaas (radi Allahu
anhu): Once the Prophet (Salallahu
alayhi was salam) embraced me and
said,

"O Allaah! Bestow on him the knowledge of
the Book (Qur'aan)."

24. Narrated by Anas (radi Allahu anhu):

Whenever the Prophet (Salallahu alayhi was salam) asked permission to enter, he knocked the door thrice with greeting and whenever he spoke a sentence (said a thing) he used to repeat it thrice.

25. Narrated by 'Ali (radi Allahu anhu): The Prophet (Salallahu alayhi was salam) said,

"Do not tell a lie against me for whoever tells a lie against me (intentionally) then he will surely enter the Hell-fire."

26. Narrated by Abu Hurayrah (radi Allahu anhu):

There is none among the Companions of the Prophet (Salallahu alayhi was salam) who has narrated more hadiths than I, except 'Abdullaah bin Amr (bin Al-'As); he used to write them and I didn't.

Hadiths from the Book of Ablutions (Wudoo'):

27. Narrated by Abu Hurayrah (radi Allahu anhu): The Prophet (Salallahu alayhi was salam) said,

"The prayer of a person who does *hadath* (passes urine, stool or wind) is not accepted till he performs (repeats) the ablution." A person from Hadaramout asked Abu Hurayrah, "What is *'hadath'*?" Abu Hurayrah replied, "'Hadath' means the passing of gas."

28. Narrated by 'Abbaas bin Tamim (radi Allahu anhu):

My uncle asked the Prophet (Salallahu alayhi was salam) about a person who imagined to have passed wind during the prayer. Allaah's Apostle replied: "He should not leave his prayers unless he hears sound or smells something."

29. Narrated by Anas (radi Allahu anhu): Whenever the Prophet (Salallahu alayhi was salam) went to answer the call of nature, he used to say,

"Allaahumma innee a'oothu bika minal-khubuthi walkhabaa'ith, i.e., O Allaah, I seek refuge with You from all offensive and wicked things (evil deeds and evil spirits)."

30. Narrated by Abu Ayyoob Al-Ansari (radi Allahu anhu): The Prophet (Salallahu alayhi was salam) said,

"If anyone of you goes to an open space for answering the call of nature he should neither face nor turn his back towards the Qiblah; he should either face the east or the west."

31. Narrated by Abu Qatadah (radi Allahu anhu): The Prophet (Salallahu alayhi was salam) said,

"Whenever any one of you drinks water, he should not breathe in the drinking utensil, and whenever any one of you goes to a lavatory, he should not touch his private parts with his right hand."

32. Narrated by Um-'Atiya (radi Allahu anhu): The Prophet (Salallahu alayhi was salam) at the time of washing his deceased daughter had said to them,

"Start from the right side beginning with those parts which are washed in ablution."

33. Narrated by 'Aishah (radi Allahu anhu):

The Prophet (Salallahu alayhi was salam) used to like to start from the right side when putting on his shoes, combing his hair, cleaning or washing himself and on doing anything else.

34. Narrated by Abu Hurayrah (radi Allahu anhu): The Prophet (Salallahu alayhi was salam) said,

"If a dog drinks from the utensil of any one of you it is essential to wash it seven times."

35. Narrated by 'Abdullaah bin 'Abbaas (radi Allahu anhu):

The Prophet (Salallahu alayhi was salam) ate a piece of cooked mutton from the shoulder region and prayed without repeating ablution.

36. Narrated by Ibn 'Abbaas (radi Allahu anhu):

The Prophet (Salallahu alayhi was salam) drank milk, rinsed his mouth and said, "It has fat."

37. Narrated by Anas (radi Allahu anhu): The Prophet (Salallahu alayhi was salam) said,

"If anyone of you feels drowsy while praying, he should sleep till he understands what he is saying (reciting)."

38. Narrated by Abu Hurayrah (radi Allahu anhu):

A Bedouin stood up and started urinating in the mosque. The people caught him but the Prophet (Salallahu alayhi was salam) ordered them to leave him and to pour a bucket or a tumbler of water over the place where he had passed the urine. The Prophet then said, "You have been sent to make things easy and not to make them difficult."

39. Narrated by 'Aishah (radi Allahu anhu) (the mother of faithful believers):

A child was brought to the Prophet (Salallahu alayhi was salam) and it urinated on the garment of the Prophet. The Prophet asked for water and poured it over the soiled place.

40. Narrated by 'Aishah (radi Allahu anhu):

The Prophet (Salallahu alayhi was salam) said, "All drinks that produce intoxication are haraam (forbidden to drink).

41. Narrated by Hudhayfah (radi Allahu anhu):

Whenever the Prophet (Salallahu alayhi was salam) got up at night, he used to clean his mouth with *siwaak*.

Hadiths from the Book of Rubbing Hands and Feet with Dust (Tayammum)'

42. Narrated by 'Ammaar (radi Allahu anhu):

The Prophet (Salallahu alayhi was salam) stroked the earth with his hands and then passed them over his face and the backs of his hands (while demonstrating *tayammum*).

43. Narrated by 'Imraan bin Husayn Al-Khuza'l (radi Allahu anhu):

The Prophet (Salallahu alayhi was salam) saw a person sitting aloof and not praying with the people. He asked him, "O so and so! What prevented you from offering the prayer with the people?" He replied, "O Allah's Apostle! I am *junub* and there is no water." The Prophet (Salallahu alayhi was salam) said, "Perform *tayammum* with clean earth and that will be sufficient for you."

Hadiths from the Book of Prayers (Salaat)

44. Narrated by 'Aishah (radi Allahu anhu), the mother of believers:

Allaah enjoined the prayer; when He enjoined it, it was two *rakaat* only (in every prayer) both when in residence or on journey. Then the prayers offered on journey remained the same, but (the *rakaat* of) the prayers for non-travelers were increased.

45. Narrated by 'Umar bin Abi Salamah (radi Allahu anhu):

In the house of Umm Salamah I saw the Prophet (Salallahu alayhi was salam) offering prayers, wrapped in a single garment around his body with its ends crossed round his shoulders.

46. Narrated by 'Aishah (radi Allahu anhu):

The Prophet (Salallahu alayhi was salam) used to offer the Fajr prayer and some believing women covered with their veiling sheets used to attend the Fajr prayer with him and then they would return to their homes unrecognized.

47. Narrated by Abu Maslama (radi Allahu anhu):

Said bin Yazid Al-Azdi said: I asked Anas bin Maalik whether the Prophet had ever prayed with his shoes on. He replied, "Yes."

48. Narrated by Anas bin Maalik (radi Allahu anhu): The Prophet (Salallahu alayhi was salam) said,

"A faithful believer while in prayer is speaking in private to his Lord, so he should neither spit in front of him nor to his right side, but he could spit either on his left or under his foot."

49. Narrated by Anas bin Maalik (radi Allahu anhu):

The Prophet (Salallahu alayhi was salam) said, "Spitting in the mosque is a sin and its expiation is to bury it."

50. Narrated by 'Aishah (radi Allahu anhu):

The Prophet (Salallahu alayhi was salam) used to start every thing from the right (for good things) whenever it was possible in all his affairs; for example: in washing, combing or wearing shoes.

51. Narrated by Abu Rafi (radi Allahu anhu):

I offered the 'Isha prayer behind Abu Hurayrah and he recited Idhas-Sama' Un-Shaqqat, and prostrated. I said, "What is this?" Abu Hurayrah said, "I prostrated behind Abu-l-Qasim and I will do the same till I meet him."

52. Narrated by 'Abdullaah bin 'Abbaas (radi Allahu anhu):

The sun eclipsed and the Prophet (Salallahu alayhi was salam) offered the eclipse prayer and said, "I have been shown the Hellfire (now) and I never seen a worse and horrible sight than the sight I have seen today."

53. Narrated by Ibn 'Umar (radi Allahu anhu):

The Prophet (Salallahu alayhi was salam) said, "Offer some of your prayers (*nawaafil*) at home, and do not take your houses as graves."

54. Narrated by Abu Qatadah Al-Aslami (radi Allahu anhu):

The Prophet (Salallahu alayhi was salam) said, "If any one of you enters a mosque, he should pray two *rakaat* before sitting."

55. Narrated by Abu Musa (radi Allahu anhu):

The Prophet (Salallahu alayhi was salam) said, "A faithful believer to a faithful believer is like the bricks of a wall, enforcing each other." While (saying that) the Prophet clasped his hands, by interlacing his fingers.

Hadiths from the Book of Virtues of the Prayer Hall (Sutra of the Musalla)

56. Narrated by Anas Ibn Maalik (radi Allahu anhu):

Whenever the Prophet (Salallahu alayhi was salam) went to answer the call of nature, me and another boy used to go after him with a staff, a stick or an *'anza* and a tumbler of water; and when he finished from answering the call of nature we would hand that tumbler of water to him.

57. Narrated by Anas (radi Allahu anhu):

I saw the most famous people amongst the Companions of the Prophet (Salallahu alayhi was salam) hurrying towards the pillars at the Maghrib prayer before the Prophet came for the prayer.

58. Narrated by 'Aishah (radi Allahu anhu):

The Prophet (Salallahu alayhi was salam) used to pray while I was sleeping across his bed in front of him. Whenever he wanted to pray *witr*, he would wake me up and I would pray *witr*.

Hadiths from the Book of Times of the Prayers

59. Narrated by Jarir bin 'Abdullaah (radi Allahu anhu):

I gave the pledge of allegiance to the Prophet (Salallahu alayhi was salam) to offer prayers perfectly, to pay Zakat regularly, and to give good advice to every Muslim.

60. Narrated by 'Aishah (radi Allahu anhu):

The Prophet (Salallahu alayhi was salam) used to pray the 'Asr prayers at a time when the sunshine was still inside my chamber and no shadow had yet appeared in it.

61.   Narrated by Ibn 'Umar (radi Allahu anhu):

The Prophet (Salallahu alayhi was salam) said, "Whoever misses the 'Asr prayer (intentionally) then it is as if he lost his family and property."

62.   Narrated by Abu Al-Mahh (radi Allahu anhu):

We were with Buraydah in a battle on a cloudy day and he said, "Offer the 'Asr prayer early as the Prophet (Salallahu alayhi was salam) said, 'Whoever leaves the 'Asr prayer, all his (good) deeds will be annulled.'"

63.   Narrated by Salamah (radi Allahu anhu):

We used to pray the Maghrib prayer with the Prophet (Salallahu alayhi was salam) when the sun disappeared from the horizon.

64.   Narrated by Abu Barza (radi Allahu anhu):

The Prophet (Salallahu alayhi was salam) disliked to sleep before the 'Isha prayer and to talk after it.

65. Narrated by 'Umar (radi Allahu anhu):

"The Prophet (Salallahu alayhi was salam) forbade praying after the Fajr prayer till the sun rises and after the 'Asr prayer till the sun sets."

66. Narrated by Ibn 'Umar (radi Allahu anhu):

The Prophet (Salallahu alayhi was salam) said, "None of you should try to pray at sunrise or sunset."

Hadiths from the Book of Call to Prayers (Adhaan)

67. Narrated by Anas (radi Allahu anhu):

Bilaal was ordered to repeat the wording of the Adhaan for prayers twice, and to pronounce the wording of the Iqaamah once except *"Qad-qamat-is-Salaat"*.

68.   Narrated by Abu Sa'eed Al-Khudri (radi Allahu anhu):

The Prophet (Salallahu alayhi was salam) said, "Whenever you hear the Adhaan, say what the Mu'adhdhin is saying.

69.   Narrated by 'Aishah (radi Allahu anhu):

The Prophet (Salallahu alayhi was salam) used to offer two light *rakaat* between the Adhaan and the Iqaamah of the Fajr prayer.

70.   Narrated by Maalik bin Huwayrith (radi Allahu anhu):

Two men came to the Prophet (Salallahu alayhi was salam) with the intention of going on a journey. The Prophet (Salallahu alayhi was salam) said, "When (both of) you set out, pronounce Adhaan and then Iqaamah and the oldest of you should lead the prayer."

71.   Narrated by 'Aun bin Abi Juhaifa (radi Allahu anhu):

My father said, "I saw Bilaal turning his face from side to side while pronouncing the Adhaan for the prayer."

72. Narrated by 'Abdullaah bin 'Umar (radi Allahu anhu):

The Prophet (Salallahu alayhi was salam) said, "The prayer in congregation is twenty seven times superior to the prayer offered by a person alone."

73. Narrated by 'Aishah (radi Allahu anhu):

The Prophet (Salallahu alayhi was salam) said, "If supper is served, and the Iqaamah is pronounced one should start with the supper."

74. Narrated by Al-Aswad (radi Allahu anhu):

I asked 'Aishah, "What did the Prophet used to do in his house?"
She replied, "He used to keep himself busy serving his family and when it was time for prayer he would go for it."

75. Narrated by Abu Hurayrah (radi Allahu anhu):

The Prophet (Salallahu alayhi was salam) said, "Isn't he who raises his head before the Imam afraid that Allaah may transform his head into that of a donkey or his figure (face) into that of a donkey?"

76. Narrated by Anas (radi Allahu anhu):

The Prophet (Salallahu alayhi was salam) said, "Listen and obey (your chief) even if an Ethiopian whose head is like a raisin were made your chief."

77. Narrated by Anas (radi Allahu anhu):

The Prophet (Salallahu alayhi was salam) used to pray a short prayer (in congregation) but used to offer it in a perfect manner.

78. Narrated by Anas bin Maalik (radi Allahu anhu):

The Prophet (Salallahu alayhi was salam) said, "Straighten your rows as the straightening of rows is essential for a perfect and correct prayer."

Hadiths from the Book of Characteristics of Prayer

79. Narrated by 'Aishah (radi Allahu anhu):

I asked the Prophet (Salallahu alayhi was salam) about looking around in prayer. He replied, "It is a way of stealing by which Satan takes away (a portion) from the prayer of a person."

80. Narrated by 'Ubadah bin As-Saamit (radi Allahu anhu):

The Prophet (Salallahu alayhi was salam) said, "Whoever does not recite Al-Faatihah in his prayer, his prayer is invalid."

81. Narrated by Abu Hurayrah (radi Allahu anhu):

The Prophet (Salallahu alayhi was salam) said, "If any one of you says, "Ameen" and the angels in the heavens say "Ameen" and the former coincides with the latter, all his past sins will be forgiven."

82. Narrated by Samurah bin Jundub (radi Allahu anhu):

The Prophet (Salallahu alayhi was salam) used to face us on completion of the prayer.

83. Narrated by Ibn 'Umar (radi Allahu anhu):

During the Battle of Khaybar the Prophet (Salallahu alayhi was salam) said, "Whoever ate from this plant (i.e., garlic) should not enter our mosque."

84. Narrated by Abu Sa'eed Al-Khudri (radi Allahu anhu):

The Prophet (Salallahu alayhi was salam) said, "Ghusl (taking a bath) on Friday is compulsory for every Muslim reaching the age of puberty."

85. Narrated by Ibn 'Umar (radi Allahu anhu):

The Prophet (Salallahu alayhi was salam) said, "If your women ask permission to go to the mosque at night, allow them."

86. Narrated by 'Abdullaah bin 'Umar (radi Allahu anhu):

The Prophet (Salallahu alayhi was salam) said, "Any one of you attending the Friday (prayers) should take a bath."

87. Narrated by Abu Hurayrah (radi Allahu anhu):

The Prophet (Salallahu alayhi was salam) said, "If I had not found it hard for my followers or the people, I would have ordered them to clean their teeth with *siwaak* for every prayer."

88. Narrated by Hudhayfah (radi Allahu anhu):

When the Prophet (Salallahu alayhi was salam) got up at night (for the night prayer), he used to clean his mouth.

89. Narrated by Anas bin Maalik (radi Allahu anhu):

The Prophet (Salallahu alayhi was salam) used to offer the Jum'uah prayer immediately after mid-day.

90. Narrated by 'Abdullaah Ibn 'Umar (radi Allahu anhu):

The Prophet (Salallahu alayhi was salam) used to deliver two Khutbahs and sit in between them.

91. Narrated by Jaabir bin 'Abdullaah (radi Allahu anhu):

A person entered the mosque while the Prophet was delivering the Khutbah on a Friday. The Prophet (Salallahu alayhi was salam) said to him, "Have you prayed?" The man replied in the negative. The Prophet (Salallahu alayhi was salam) said, "Get up and pray two *rakaat*."

92. Narrated by Anas (radi Allahu anhu):

We used to offer the Jum'uah prayer early and then have the afternoon nap.

Hadiths from the Book of The Two Festivals (Eids)

93. Narrated by Anas bin Maalik (radi Allahu anhu):

The Prophet (Salallahu alayhi was salam) never proceeded (for the prayer) on the Day of 'Eid-ul-Fitr unless he had eaten some dates. Anas also narrated: The Prophet used to eat odd number of dates.

Hadith from the Book of Witr Prayer

94. Narrated by 'Aishah (radi Allahu anhu):

The Prophet (Salallahu alayhi was salam) offered *witr* prayer at different nights at various hours extending (from the 'Isha prayer) up to the last hour of the night.

Hadiths from the Book of Invoking Allaah for Rain (Istisqaa)

95. Narrated by 'Aishah (radi Allahu anhu):

Whenever the Prophet (Salallahu alayhi was salam) saw the rain, he used to say, "O Allaah! Let it be a strong, fruitful rain."

96. Narrated by Anas (radi Allahu anhu):

Whenever a strong wind blew, anxiety appeared on the face of the Prophet (fearing that wind might be a sign of Allaah's wrath).

97. Narrated by Ibn Abbaas (radi Allahu anhu):

The Prophet (Salallahu alayhi was salam) said, "I was granted victory with As-Saba and the nation of 'Aad was destroyed by Ad-Dabur (westerly wind).

98. Narrated by Abu Masood (radi Allahu anhu):

The Prophet (Salallahu alayhi was salam) said, "The sun and the moon do not eclipse because of the death of someone from the people but they are two signs amongst the signs of Allaah; when you see them stand up and pray."

Hadiths from the Book of Prostration during Recital of Qur'aan

99. Narrated by Ibn 'Umar (radi Allahu anhu):

When the Prophet (Salallahu alayhi was salam) recited Soorat As-Sajdah and we were with him, he would prostrate and we would also prostrate with him; and some of us (because of the heavy rush) would not find a place (for our foreheads) to prostrate on.

100. Narrated by Ibn 'Umar (radi Allahu anhu):

Whenever the Prophet (Salallahu alayhi was salam) recited the Soorah which contained the prostration of recitation he used to prostrate and then, we too, would prostrate; and some of us did not find a place for prostration.

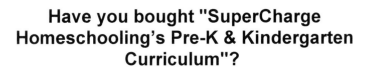

Have you bought "SuperCharge Homeschooling's Pre-K & Kindergarten Curriculum"?

Pre-K Curriculum

Kindergarten Curriculum

Have You Bought the Series "Things Every Kid Should Know: Drugs, Alcohol, Smoking, Bullying and Junk Food" for Your Kids By An "11 Year Old" Author, Alya Nuri

Have You Bought the Series: "Things Every Kid Should Know: Strangers, Fire and Reduce, Reuse & Recycle" for Your Kids By A "8 Year Old" Author, Zafar Nuri?

Have You Bought the Series "Things Every Kid Should Know: Hand Washing" for Your Kids By A "6 Year Old" Author, Arsalon Nuri

CPSIA information can be obtained
at www.ICGtesting.com
Printed in the USA
BVHW020755030322
630444BV00006B/5

* 9 7 8 1 9 3 5 9 4 8 2 0 9 *